My Book of Words

Illustrated by Heather Heyworth

WINDMILL
BOOKS

At home

bedroom

curtains

bed

drawers

closet

kitchen

refrigerator

cupboards

stove

What color are the curtains in the bedroom?

2

bathroom

toilet

sink

bathtub

television

window

door

sofa

living room

How many of these objects do you have in your home?

3

In the home

pillow

lamp

clock

telephone

chair

book

table

4

Can you name the animal on the lamp?

Toys

puzzle

car

teddy bear

train

doll

dinosaur

blocks

What are your favorite toys to play with?

In the garden

fence

shed

strawberries

carrots

bee

dog

caterpillar

leaf

grass

6

How many carrots are growing in the garden?

clothesline

bird

bush

ball

tree

butterfly

flowers

cat

What other things might be in a garden?

In the family

Grandpa

Grandma

Daddy

Mommy

baby

sister

brother

How many people are there in this family?

My body

head
ear
nose
mouth
arm
tummy
hand
eye
toes

hair
face
teeth
fingers
knee
leg
foot

Can you point to these parts of your body?

9

On the street

park

bus

house

bus stop

car

crosswalk

motorcycle

road

10

What color is the car?

Which stores do you like best?

Things that go

airplane

hot-air balloon

train

truck

tractor

How many of these vehicles can fly?

ambulance

helicopter

digger

ferry

fire engine

yacht

Which of these vehicles have you seen?

13

At the park

sky

kite

boat

path

pond

bicycle

ducks

picnic

ice cream

blanket

How many ducks can you see?

cloud

squirrel

bench

slide

swings

What do you like to do at the park?

15

Picnic food

bread

cookies

cup

eggs

sandwiches

plate

cake

spoon

fork

knife

juice

What food do you like to eat on a picnic?

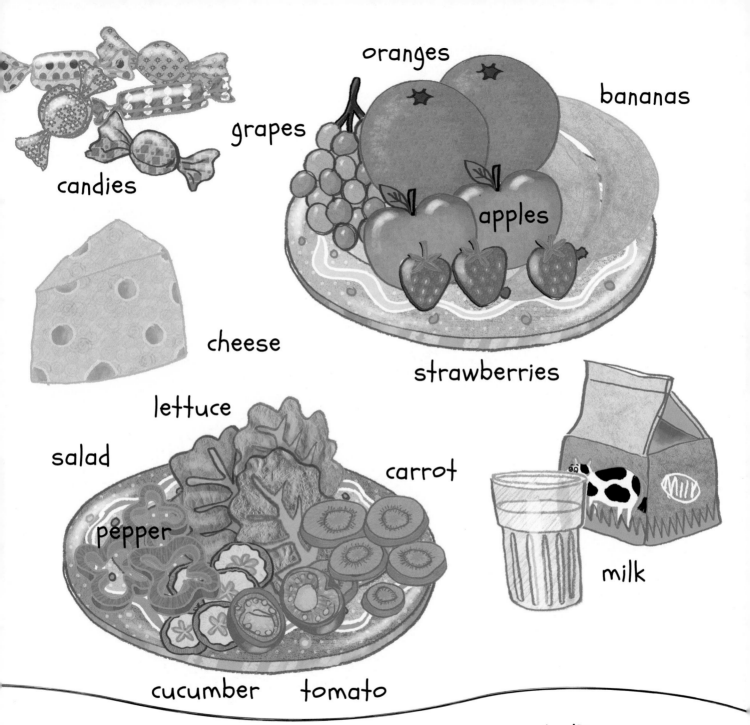

candies

grapes

oranges

bananas

apples

cheese

strawberries

lettuce

salad

carrot

pepper

milk

cucumber   tomato

How many different foods are in the salad?

On the beach

gull

sea

boat

shovel

sandcastle

boy

bucket

shell

How many shells can you find?

sun

waves

crab

girl

towel

starfish

sand

sunglasses

What do you like doing on the beach?

19

Clothes

shorts

sweater

dress

T-shirt

socks

scarf

skirt

gloves

underwear

coat

undershirt

shoes

pants

Which of these clothes do you wear when it is cold?

Colors

black

green

yellow

blue

red

pink

brown

purple

orange

white

What color clothes are you wearing?

Shapes

triangle

square

circle

rectangle

star

oval

diamond

heart

What shape is an egg?

Numbers

one

two

three

four

five

six

seven

eight

nine

ten

Can you count all the way from one to twenty?

Can you find?

Look back in your book to see if you can find the following things.

clock

teddy bear

dinosaur

hot-air balloon

sandwiches

yacht

candies

T-shirt

Published in 2019 by Windmill Books,
an Imprint of Rosen Publishing
29 East 21st Street, New York, NY 10010

Copyright © 2019 Miles Kelly Publishing

Cataloging-in-Publication Data

Names: Heyworth, Heather, illustrator.
Title: Words / illustrated by Heather Heyworth.
Description: New York : Windmill Books, 2019. | Series: My book of

Identifiers: ISBN 9781508196563 (pbk.) | ISBN 9781508196556 (library bound) | ISBN 9781508196570 (6 pack)
Subjects: LCSH: Vocabulary–Pictorial works–Juvenile literature. | Vocabulary–Juvenile literature.
Classification: LCC PE1449.H49 2019 | DDC 428.1–dc23

Manufactured in the United States of America

CPSIA Compliance Information: Batch BS18WM: For Further Information contact Rosen Publishing, New York, New York at 1-800-237-9932

For web resources related to the subject of this book, go to: www.windmillbooks.com/weblinks and select this book's title.